Energy for Today

Ethanol
and Other New Fuels

By Tea Benduhn

Reading consultant: Susan Nations, M.Ed.,
author/literacy coach/consultant in literacy development

Science and curriculum consultant: Debra Voege, M.A.,
science curriculum resource teacher

WEEKLY READER®
PUBLISHING

Please visit our web site at www.garethstevens.com.
For a free color catalog describing our list of high-quality books,
call 1-800-542-2595 (USA) or 1-800-387-3178 (Canada). Our fax: 1-877-542-2596

Library of Congress Cataloging-in-Publication Data

Benduhn, Tea.
    Energy for today : ethanol and other new fuels / by Tea Benduhn.
       p. cm. — (Weekly reader books)
    Includes bibliographical references and index.
    ISBN-10: 0-8368-9260-7 — ISBN-13: 978-0-8368-9260-4 (lib. bdg.)
    ISBN-10: 0-8368-9359-X — ISBN-13: 978-0-8368-9359-5 (softcover)
    1. Alcohol as fuel—Juvenile literature. 2. Fuel—Juvenile literature.
  3. Power resources—Juvenile literature. I. Title.
  TP358.B38   2009
  662'.6692—dc22   2008014483

This edition first published in 2009 by
Weekly Reader® Books
An Imprint of Gareth Stevens Publishing
1 Reader's Digest Road
Pleasantville, NY 10570-7000 USA

Senior Managing Editor: Lisa M. Herrington
Senior Editor: Brian Fitzgerald
Creative Director: Lisa Donovan
Designer: Ken Crossland
Photo Researcher: Diane Laska-Swanke
Special thanks to Kirsten Weir

Image credits: Cover and title page: © Don Farrall/Getty Images; pp. 5, 7: © Photos.com/Jupiterimages Unlimited;
p. 6: © John Klein/Weekly Reader; p. 9: © iStockphoto.com; p. 10: © Sai Yeung Chan/Shutterstock; p. 11: © John Shaw/
Photo Researchers, Inc.; p. 12: © Pasquale Sorrentino/Photo Researchers, Inc.; p. 13: © Hougaard Malan/Shutterstock;
p. 15: © Bobbi Lane/Weekly Reader; p. 16: © Carolina K. Smith, M.D./Shutterstock; p. 17: © Mark Boulton/Photo
Researchers, Inc.; p. 18: © ETH Zurich; p. 19: © Nilo Lima/Photo Researchers, Inc.; p. 21: © Corbis RF/Alamy

Printed in the United States

1 2 3 4 5 6 7 8 9 10 09 08

Table of Contents

Words that appear in the glossary are printed in **boldface** type the first time they occur in the text.

Chapter 1

What Are Ethanol and Other New Fuels?

Can you imagine a car that runs on corn? That might sound like a crazy idea. In fact, many cars already get their power from corn. Ethanol is a type of fuel made from corn or other plants. Ethanol is added to the gasoline we put in our cars.

Ethanol is a type of **alcohol**. Alcohol is made from sugars in plants. Sugar gives corn its sweet flavor. Almost all plants contain sugars—even plants we don't eat. People can make ethanol from many plants besides corn. Soybeans, grass, and wood can all be turned into ethanol. In Brazil, people use sugarcane to make ethanol.

Corn is not just food. It is also used as a source of fuel!

Ethanol is not the only fuel made from plants. **Biodiesel** is also made from plants. Most plants contain oils. Biodiesel is made from plant oils.

More than 100 years ago, an inventor named Rudolph Diesel created an engine that used vegetable oil as fuel. The diesel engine became popular, but using vegetable oil for fuel did not catch on. In recent years, though, people have started using biodiesel again.

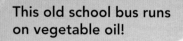

This old school bus runs on vegetable oil!

Water can be found almost anywhere on Earth. If scientists could make it work, water would be a great source of fuel.

Ethanol and biodiesel are new fuels made from plants. Some inventors are trying to make new fuels from a different source—water! Water can be used to make a type of fuel called **hydrogen fuel cells**. Car engines that run on fuel cells are very expensive to make. But many people are working to make fuel cells better. They hope that hydrogen will be the fuel of the future.

Chapter 2

Sources of Energy

What's so special about fuel? Fuel is used for **energy**. Energy is the ability to move people and things. There are different kinds of energy. When you're sitting still, you are filled with energy that you aren't using. That stored energy is called **potential energy**. When you stand up and walk, your potential energy becomes **kinetic energy**, or moving energy. Fuel is potential energy. It stores energy to power cars and planes.

Fossil fuels can be hard to reach. An oil drill pumps oil from deep underground.

Today, most cars and trucks get energy from gasoline. Gasoline is made from oil pumped from the ground. Oil is a **fossil fuel**. It formed from the remains of plants and animals that lived millions of years ago. Coal and natural gas are also fossil fuels. Fossil fuels are **nonrenewable resources**. Once they are used up, they can never be replaced.

We burn fossil fuels to release their energy. Most cars get their power by burning gasoline. Burning fossil fuels also creates **pollution**. Pollution is harmful materials in the air, water, or soil. Polluted air is hard to breathe. Every day, people burn huge amounts of fossil fuels for energy.

Air pollution hangs over many major cities, including Los Angeles, California.

As Earth heats up, polar bears and other animals that need the cold could lose their homes.

You may have heard of **global warming**. The temperature of Earth is slowly rising. Most scientists say that pollution from burning fossil fuels is causing Earth to warm up. Global warming can change the way we live. Scientists say global warming will make ice disappear from cold places, such as the North Pole. Global warming can also change the weather and make more storms.

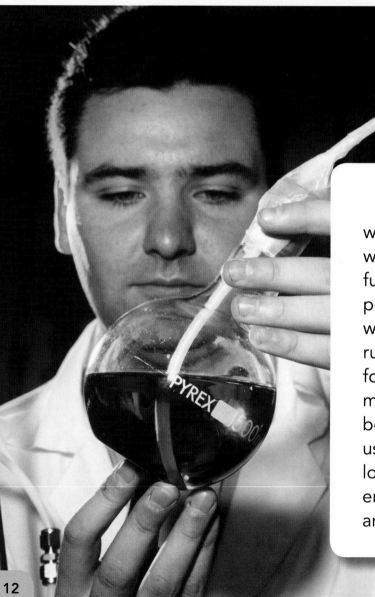

Scientists are working on new ways to use plants as fuels.

Many people are worried about global warming. They want fuels that will not make pollution. They also want fuels that will not run out. Every year, fossil fuels become more expensive because they are being used up. Scientists are looking for sources of energy that are clean and will not run out.

Why are corn and other plants a good source of fuel? Plants are a **renewable resource**. They are a source of energy that can be replaced. When we use plants, we can grow more to replace them. Plants also help make the air clean. Plants give off the **oxygen** that we breathe. We need oxygen to live. We can make fuel from plants. Scientists must find ways to turn plants into fuel without making pollution.

Oxygen from plants gives us the energy we need to live.

Chapter 3

How New Fuels Work

People have used plants for fuel for thousands of years. They burned wood for heat and to cook food. They even used plant oils in lamps to light rooms. Much later, some of the first cars ever built ran on fuel made from vegetable oil. Today, we still use plants for fuel in some of these ways.

Plants get energy from sugars. To make sugar, plants need a gas from the air called **carbon dioxide**. Too much carbon dioxide in the air is bad for the environment. It leads to global warming. Burning fossil fuels gives off a lot of carbon dioxide. Burning plant fuels gives off less carbon dioxide. Some scientists say that using plants for fuel will slow global warming.

We give off carbon dioxide when we breathe. Plants use carbon dioxide to make sugars.

More and more cars are being made to run on fuel that is 85 percent ethanol.

To make plants into fuel, scientists use **yeast**. Yeast feeds on plants. It turns their sugars into ethanol. People mix ethanol with gasoline. Most cars run on a mix of 10 percent ethanol with 90 percent gasoline. Some cars are designed to run on fuel that is mostly ethanol. It has just a little bit of gas mixed in it. Using more ethanol cuts down on pollution.

16

Like ethanol, biodiesel must be mixed with fossil fuels to work well. Plant oils get thicker when they are cool. Thick oil can damage a car's engine. Mixing plant oils with fossil fuels helps them stay thin and runny. Some cars today have diesel engines. They run on diesel fuel made from fossil fuels. People can buy special kits to change those cars to run on biodiesel instead.

Some cars can be changed to run on biodiesel fuel made from vegetable oil.

Fuels made from plants might be good sources of energy. Fuel made from hydrogen may be even better. Hydrogen fuel cells can store a lot of energy. Hydrogen fuel does not make any pollution. It does not give off any carbon dioxide. Making hydrogen fuel cells is difficult, though. We can get hydrogen from water, but doing so is very expensive.

This test car runs on a hydrogen fuel cell. It makes no pollution and can go thousands of miles on a single gallon of gasoline.

Chapter 4

New Fuels in the Future

What fuels will power our future? One day, ethanol, hydrogen, and other new fuels may replace fossil fuels. Some people are starting to use these fuels already. In the future, we will need to use even more new fuels. Today, it is expensive to make ethanol and biodiesel. It is even more expensive to make hydrogen fuel cells. Scientists are working to create the best new fuels for the future.

Making fuel from plants is not perfect. We need to grow a lot of corn or other crops to make plant fuels. People also need corn and soybeans for food. To grow enough plants for fuel, we need a lot of land. Also, ethanol and biodiesel produce much less energy than gasoline does. Before ethanol and biodiesel can replace fossil fuels, we need a better way to turn plants into fuel.

Growing plants for fuel uses a lot of land. Should rain forests be cut down so people can grow sugarcane or soybeans for ethanol?

Many scientists are working to create new fuels for the future. For now, most of our energy still comes from fossil fuels. So how can we prevent pollution and global warming? We can use less energy. We can walk or ride bikes instead of driving. We can read books instead of watching TV. No matter where our fuel comes from in the future, saving energy will always be a bright idea.

You can save energy by riding a bike instead of riding in a car.

Glossary

alcohol: a substance made from plant sugars that can be used for fuel

biodiesel: a type of fuel made from plant oils

carbon dioxide: a gas that plants need to make sugar. People and animals give off carbon dioxide when they breathe out.

energy: the ability to do work

fossil fuel: a source of energy, such as oil, gas, or coal, that formed from the remains of plants or animals that lived millions of years ago

global warming: the slow rise in Earth's temperature

hydrogen fuel cells: a type of fuel made from a substance found in water

kinetic energy: energy that is moving

nonrenewable resources: resources that cannot be used again. Once they are used, they are gone forever. Fossil fuels are nonrenewable resources.

oxygen: a gas that all animals need to stay alive

pollution: harmful materials in the environment

potential energy: energy that is stored

renewable resource: a resource that can be used again. Renewable resources include air, water, sunlight, wind, and plants and animals.

yeast: a tiny animal that eats plant sugars and makes them into alcohol

To Find Out More

Books

Air Pollution. Science Matters (series). Heather C. Hudak (Weigl Publishers, 2006)

Amazing Plants. Amazing Life Cycles (series). Honor Head (Gareth Stevens, 2008)

Hydrogen: Running on Water. Energy Revolution (series). Niki Walker (Crabtree, 2007)

Web Sites

Kaboom! Energy

tiki.oneworld.net/energy/energy.html

Learn about many sources of energy, including plant fuels and fuel cells.

Science News For Kids

www.sciencenewsforkids.org/articles/20060412/Feature1.asp

Find out more about ethanol and some wild ideas for creating new fuels.

Publisher's note to educators and parents: Our editors have carefully reviewed these web sites to ensure that they are suitable for children. Many web sites change frequently, however, and we cannot guarantee that a site's future contents will continue to meet our high standards of quality and educational value. Be advised that children should be closely supervised whenever they access the Internet.

Index

About the Author

Tea Benduhn writes books and edits a magazine. She lives in the beautiful state of Wisconsin with her husband and two cats. The walls of their home are lined with bookshelves filled with books. Tea says, "I read every day. It is more fun than watching television!"